FAYE and ME, A MEMOIR

by

Allan Ishmael Young

Available from
ALLAN YOUNG
CANNON PUBLISHING COMPANY
4430 Bauer Farm Drive, Ste. 128
Lawrence, KS 66049
allanishmaelyoung@gmail.com

FAYE and ME, A MEMOIR
by Allan Ishmael Young

CHAPTER ONE, St. Charles Girl

I had gone up to St. Charles on an errand for my father that summer day, something I did often, being sixteen and having a driver's license. This day had remained late to visit friends. I knew a few of the high school students who were sons and daughters of friends of my folks. And of course I had relatives, boys and girls, in Bonny Blue, one of the coal camps.

During the course of my wanderings around the town, I ran into my cousin Howard, who said, "Remember my friend Darrell Honeycutt? I'm going down to a gathering at his house in Wagner Town. Want to come along?"

I remembered Darrell, a good-looking guy in his late teens, who seemed to be inseparable from Howard. Having nothing better to do, I agreed to go.

As we walked across a small footbridge to a house that sat between the railroad and the creek, I could see from a distance, even though it was almost dark, that there were several boys and girls on the front porch. As I was being introduced to Howard's friends, and greeting some that I already knew, I heard someone say "Hi" with such a sweet, female voice that I immediately hoped she was talking to me. I turned around and saw, sitting on the banister in the dusk being lighted by the rising moon, what was, without a doubt, the prettiest girl I had ever seen in my sixteen years!

I said "Hi," and just stood and looked at her, after awhile feeling like a total idiot. She was simply smiling at me, across the darkened porch, and I didn't know whether she was being derisive or whether she really liked my looks. Getting closer as someone turned on a porch light, I could see that she had long dark brown hair and exotic bright blue eyes, the kind you just fall in and swim around, and I immediately started swimming for my life. I had never noticed girls' eyes before—couldn't even remember the color of the eyes of most of the girls I knew. But hers were different. She looked striking in a royal blue skirt and a white blouse, topping brown loafers and white anklets. The shape of her calf muscles was appealing to this teenager immediately. But no matter what she had been wearing, she would have looked like a royal princess. The magic aura which surrounded her enveloped me completely. Suddenly feeling like a fool for just staring at her, I stumbled back across the porch to where Darrell and Howard were talking.

"Who is that?" I blurted out, looking back towards the girl.

"Oh, her? She's my kid sister, Faye," said Darrell. "I'm surprised you don't know her. She will be a senior this year, like you. And you seem to know a lot of these other girls, like Helen Carter and Joy Osborne, who are close friends of hers."

Feeling bolder, and armed with this knowledge, I tiptoed across the porch and sat down beside her on the railing.

She was chatting with somebody, but when she looked around at me, I said, "Good evening, Miss Honeycutt."

"My, aren't you the formal one, though, Mr. Young," she said in that musical voice that had entranced me earlier—even sweeter, now that it was directed at me.

"Apparently you know my name," I said. "I have to admit I had to ask your brother who you were."

"These girls told me," she said. "I had to ask them, too."

"Call me Ishmael," I said, "like the narrator in Moby Dick. I'll spell it if you like."

"No need, Ishmael," she said. "I can read, and I know it's also a Biblical name. As you know by now, I'm Faye. I won't tell you what my middle name is."

"I don't care," I said. "Your first name is the most beautiful I've ever heard, and it matches its owner—especially her eyes."

"Oh, my," she said, "such a line. How many girls have you used that on? Whatever am I going to do with you?"

"I don't know any lines," I said. "I'm just stupid enough to blurt out my impressions and feelings. And as to what you are going to do with me, I hope it is a lot—whatever it is—and that it lasts a long time."

At this time some of her girl friends engaged her in conversations, and she turned her back on me—although I could see her twist her head around to look at me occasionally. I went home later knowing I was smitten—not thinking of my lost Emma Lou at all. I tried to pump Howard about her, but he seemed overly protective where she was concerned, and kept referring to her as a little kid. She didn't look like a kid to me. I did learn she worked in a drug store in St. Charles, and decided to make it a point to stop in there. The following Saturday I did so.

CHAPTER TWO, Faye and Ishmael

As I walked in she saw me and smiled, but before I could greet her, a male voice called to me to come over. It was Jim Myers' brother, Billy—known as Buddy, sitting at a small round ice cream table with two other boys I recognized from St. Charles high school. I sat down in the empty chair by them, while still watching Faye. She came over with a notepad and started asking what each of them wanted. Suddenly Buddy pulled her down on his knee, then put his arm around her while she took the orders. I was chagrined—apparently she was available to any old knee that was available.

But, I thought, *what the heck, this is not the first time I've been disappointed in a girl. But why her? I thought she was spotless.*

When she turned to me, and asked, "Did you want something, Ishmael?" I was burning.

"I did when I came in," I said, "but I don't now."

And I got up and bolted out the door.

A week later, I was in St. Charles again, when I ran into Joy Osborne. Her being my age, and the youngest daughter of my parents' one-time best friends, Jim and Maude, I had known Joy as long as I could remember. This evening she told me she was heading for a meeting of the Baptist Young People's Union at the local church. Suddenly she asked me if I would like to go along. When I hesitated, she said all they did was sing songs and play games. So I went with her.

The first person I saw when we entered the door to the church's basement meeting room was Faye. She was wearing a bright royal blue skirt with a white blouse, which made her blue eyes look even bluer. I could be wrong, but I think they got bigger when she saw me with Joy. We avoided each other all evening, me sticking close to Joy.

I saw no more of her after that evening—if anything I stayed away from places she might be, especially the St. Charles drug store. Soon the summer was over, as marked by the Lee County Fair, and it was almost time for school to start. At the end of my ticket-taking shift at the Fair on Saturday, its last day, I started wandering down the midway. Four girls, whom I had seen enter earlier—but the other ticket-taker had admitted them—accosted me. Included in those excited faces was one with swimmingly blue eyes and dark hair, easily recognizable anywhere—Faye!

After some polite conversation about what I was doing at the Fair, it came out that I had certain privileges—like free rides. Suddenly there was a chorus of voices telling me they liked rides—except that Faye's voice was noticeably absent.

"And you, Miss Honeycutt," I said, smiling at her, "I bet you are afraid of the rides."

"No," said one of the girls. "She is the one of us who will ride anything—the wilder the better."

"Then let's ride the swings," I said to her.

She smiled at me, and said, "Let's go. And I bet you throw up before I do!"

We rode many rides, and neither of us got sick. But when we rode the Ferris wheel, I didn't pull my ruse about kissing when the wheel stopped with us on top, as I had done with many girls. Somehow I was afraid it might not work on her.

So I took her hand, saying, "Can I drive you home?"

"I had better rejoin my friends," she said, as we got off the last ride, neither of us having thrown up. "My folks will be expecting me to come home with them. I might have difficulty explaining you, if you take me home—even though I would like it."

"That's OK," I said. "I understand. I have protective parents, too. Will I see you again?"

"If you'd like," she said. "But what about Joy?"

"Joy and I are nothing," I said. "I've known her all my life, and that meeting at your church was the only time we have ever done anything together—besides play with her toys when we were toddlers. What about you and Buddy?"

"Me and who?"

"Buddy. Billy Myers. I was disturbed when you sat on his knee in the drugstore."

"I hope that's not why I never saw you anymore all summer! I hardly knew any of those boys. I was so shocked I didn't know what to do. Harry, the druggist, told me later I should have just gotten up and asked him to wait on the boys. It was inappropriate behavior—on the part of the boy and me."

"I'm sorry," I said, realizing that the summer might not have seemed so long, if I hadn't reacted negatively to the incident.

"I'm sorry for what I was thinking when I saw you with Joy, too," she said.

Soon we found her friends, and we parted. I watched them go out the gate, then floated on air back to my car.

CHAPTER THREE, Fragmented Friendship

So began a fragmented friendship that lasted all summer and throughout the school year. She always looked striking in her clothes, usually a skirt and blouse or sweater. She just stood out compared to other girls. I had heard that girls avoid hanging out with one who is better-looking than they are, and would not have been surprised if that was the case with Faye.

I saw quite a bit of her in St. Charles and other places, and sometimes found myself basing my behavior on what she might think of what I was doing. But even then I was smart enough, mature enough and close enough to reality to realize what I was doing, and that she probably didn't think about me at all. Then when my senior class was invited to a nearby university to visit, I was getting off the Pennington school bus when a bus from St. Charles High pulled up alongside. I walked over to see if she was on it, and she was. Many eyebrows were being raised as I spent the day with this lovely girl whom none of my classmates had seen before.

After that I found many occasions to visit the St. Charles High School campus, and she was always there to see me whenever I did.

As my senior year of high school rapidly drew to a close, I knew full well that soon my life would be changed forever. It was common practice for the staff of the school newspaper to have a banquet somewhere, at the expense of the income from the paper, along towards the end of the year. As editor, realizing that this was probably the last big event of my school days, since I knew full well that I couldn't make it to college, I had hoped to make this a really special event, before my departure for the Navy immediately after graduation. However, it did not turn out that way.

As editor of the Monthly Splash, the high school newspaper, I looked forward to this most prestigious event of the year—the Press Banquet.

The girls were to wear evening dresses and we boys to wear suits, and meet in the dining room of the Monte Vista Hotel in Big Stone Gap, about twenty miles from Pennington. I had already decided to ask Faye, the prettiest girl in St. Charles, and everywhere else, for that matter, to go, getting the message to her through Miss Hobbs, the typing teacher, who spent mornings at Pennington High, then afternoons at St. Charles. Faye told Miss Hobbs she would like to go, but had to ask her folks—naturally. Then the next day she told Miss Hobbs her folks wouldn't let her go. I was literally heartsick. It never occurred to me to question it figuring most girls would consider it an impressive event to attend—even if they didn't like their date. Perhaps she didn't want to go, or didn't have an evening dress, or her folks wouldn't let her wear one, or it was too far from home. But no, it had to be they didn't want her to be with me.

I had wanted to take someone who was outstandingly beautiful, and who would outshine all the other girls at the banquet. Faye was the only girl I knew who fit that description. Then I realized I had done this wrong, and told Miss Hobbs so. I should have gone to Faye's house, asked her to go, then, if she indicated she wanted to, I should have asked her parents myself—telling them that there would be two teachers at the banquet.

But then Miss Hobbs told me that Faye's family had lost a younger brother, about ten years old, to a brain hemorrhage recently—so they had become very protective of their remaining two offspring. That shed a new light on the situation.

But I wasn't ready to give up on being friends with her. Right before graduation, I bought a dresser set for her, something I had learned my two sisters valued highly. Since she had no telephone, I just simply walked down to her house on Saturday carrying the gift. I met her father on the way, and he was civil—telling me hello. Faye met me at the door wearing a chenille housecoat. I had caught her before she had time to get dressed. She didn't seem embarrassed, but I was. I should have come later, but I had been afraid she might not be there. She accepted the gift graciously, and I left. I couldn't have been there more than five minutes.

Later I ran into her in St. Charles and she presented me with a billfold—which I am sure she had just bought. I left for the Navy a few days later, and did not contact her from there, or when I was home on leave, or after I was discharged. I fully expected her, as well as other girls I knew, to be married by the time I was discharged.

CHAPTER FOUR, Other Girls, Good and Bad Relationships

But during this period I thought of her a lot, although I still thought any sort of relationship would be futile. It was also a time to reminisce about other girls I had known, some were good situations, some not. It started primarily with a little neighbor who was my age.

Her name was Leafy. I thought her name was funny, but she said that's really it. I met her at the Daugherty spring my first week at Elk Knob. We were both about eight years old, and played there and then picked some apples in the orchard. I thought they were awful poor, because she did not wear any underwear, just a loose, raggedy dress. I guessed they could not afford to buy her any panties or bloomers like other girls wore.

I had seen a girl's bottom before, since I had two sisters, and we lived in a little house. But before moving there, we lived in Kemmerer Gem, a coal camp. We had a garden up on the side of a hill behind our house. Whenever my mom would send me up there to get some radishes, onions or lettuce, the neighbor girl, Jean, about my age, used to tag along. She wore a ragged dress over panties made of flour sacks by her mother, as most of the little girls there did. But as soon as we got to the garden on hot days, she took off all her clothes and hung them on a bush. Then she helped me while she was naked. She said it was too hot to wear clothes, and she tried to get me to take mine off, too. Her mother was a preacher's daughter, but maybe she never told Jean not to show her butt. I wore just bib overalls—no underwear, no socks or shoes, and no shirt. But I never took them off. If I did I might get something hung up on a bush or the fence and hurt myself.

Then one day in the orchard by the Daugherty spring, I told Leafy I liked her looks and her cute bottom. And she became even friendlier—took off her dress to show me all of her, while we climbed apple trees. So I told her I liked her friendly smile and hair. The next time she came to meet me it was too cool to get naked, but her hair was combed real nice, and she brought me a homemade cookie.

Then later there was Janie. She was in my grade at Elk Knob. She lived a short distance from us, on the same road, and began to come to our place after school and seeking me out to play catch. I complied as soon as my chores were finished, which was usually by the time she arrived. One evening when I threw the ball to her, she missed it, and it went into a ditch under some cedars. Soon she indicated she couldn't find it. When I walked up to help her look, she was sitting on a rock outcropping with her shirt unbuttoned, revealing a little pink brassiere. She usually wore very tight-fitting and revealing short shorts, but so did most girls in warm weather, away from school. Even in school, the girls wore such short skirts, and were so unladylike in their seats, that all we boys had to do was look around to be entertained by little pink panties all over the school room. I began to find it exciting, at my age, but I had two older sisters, so girls' figures were nothing new. But this was different. My naïve nature told me Janie just had trouble keeping her blouse fastened, so I just felt sorry for her. But later I decided she was probably just showing me that she was growing up, and now had something to put in her bra for it to support.

Now let me tell you about my life as a thespian, with an unintentional humorous act. I had been in school plays all my student years, but when I started high school, they were putting on a blackface minstrel show. (Can't do that, now.) I was an "Endman," one of the funny men, who responds stupidly to the questions of the white "Interlocutor." (By my senior year I was the Interlocutor—in a white tux, no less.) There was a chorus of beautiful (or not) girls in evening dresses at the rear of the stage, and an occasional solo singer, duet or dance act interjected in the program.

She had the unlikely name of "James Alyce," the daughter of one of the two richest men in town—two brothers who operated the biggest coal company in the area, among other things. Everyone loved her, this little tomboy with the pageboy hair style. Her nickname had been "Squirt" in grade school, but I did not know her then. She was assigned to sing a song to me, and during rehearsals of her song I just stood there with my back to the seats, while I worked at recalling my lines—paying little attention to her.

One of the things I had to do in the show, playing the part of a jewel thief, was to race behind the chorus girls and remove their necklaces. I practiced this diligently with the cooperation of some of the girls, getting the hang of the clasps and fasteners. At a rehearsal, the director complimented me on being so adroit at it.

Then the twisted humor side of James Alyce showed up, when she said, loudly, “You ought to see him on bra straps!”

Then, after I got my wits about me, I brazenly said, “You ought to know!”

The first performance was going well—me in a tuxedo in blackface. Then James Alyce came out to sing her song, something called, "Tall Dark and Handsome, That's the Man for Me." This little tomboy had a high fashion hairdo, and was in dark brown makeup, clear down over her half-exposed breasts. She was an absolute knockout beauty! As she finished the lines of her song, she closed in on me, and I inadvertently took a step backward, and fell off the four-foot high stage! The audience howled.

The director said, “Leave it in, leave it in,” meaning she wanted me to fall off the stage at each performance.

I did, with great trepidation. James Alyce sometimes accused me of upstaging her performance.

Good thing I didn't try Hollywood, I'd have been a cripple by age thirty!

She was fun, but my disappointment came when she told me that her mother was having a sixteenth birthday party for her, but would not let her invite the "likes of me" to it—whatever that meant. But James Alyce said she would meet me somewhere sometime and we could do something. We never did. I didn't think I could afford her.

Girls, what high school boy can understand them!

One day on the playground at the high school one of my friends suddenly said, "Look at the body on that!"

I looked around to see Irene, whom I had just met last summer. I had been on a cross-country hike on Big Hill when I came upon an elderly woman hoeing her garden in the yard of a small house beside the road. Straightening up with difficulty, she greeted me.

"I'm getting too old for this," she said, smiling.

"Nice garden, though," I said.

"I'm due a break," she said. "Want a cold drink?"

"Sure could use one," I said.

She called into the house, "Irene, bring some cold water for two people."

As we sat on the edge of a porch which ran clear across the front of the small house, a small blond, attractive girl came out and handed us each a cold glass. I thanked her, although she never looked directly at me, and she went back in the house.

"My grand daughter," said my hostess. "She is a little shy."

“I think I’ve seen her at high school,” I said.

I finished my drink, thanked the lady, and continued my hike.

At the beginning of my junior year I was at some school affair at which this same little blonde sophomore showed up. Living way up on Big Hill, she didn’t get to very many such gatherings—but this time she was spending the night with a friend. I joined them from time to time. We had fun, so the next day in school, I handed her a note saying how nice she looked the previous evening, and how much I enjoyed her company. The last note I would ever write to a girl! Within minutes, it seemed like almost everybody in school had read that note—and whoever hadn’t, had heard about it. I was ragged to death. Later Irene found me alone on the steps to the press room.

“I made a mistake, didn’t I?” she said.

“Well, at least you showed poor judgment, Irene,” I answered. “That was meant to be private.”

“Well, if that is the attitude you want to take,” she said, self-righteously, I thought, “I don’t want to be friends, anyway.”

And she stalked away. I was convinced she was just too embarrassed and didn’t know what else to do.

Helen’s closest friend was Kathryn from “across the ridge,” near Stickleyville. When the senior banquet rolled around, Helen, knowing that I was not tied down, asked me to join her and her boyfriend in a double date—mine being Kathryn, whom I hardly knew. If I would do it, Kathryn would spend the night with Helen. Of course again, I had a car. Reluctantly, I agreed—really preferring to go to the banquet alone. The first time Kathryn and I had a few seconds alone, she told me I was not to consider this a romantic date, because she had a boyfriend in the Army. Fine with me. After the dinner, Helen suggested we drive to the top of the ridge. Under any other circumstances that would have been great with me. You could park right where the highway crossed Wallins Ridge, and look out over the fog-bound moonlit valley below. Wonderful place to take your favorite girl. But this night, while Helen and her guy were warming up the back seat, my date and I just sat there. I was glad when it was time to go home. The next school day, Helen accosted me on the front walk.

"You disappointed us Friday night," Helen said. "Kathryn said you had a reputation as liking girls, but she thought you were a dud."

"I do like girls," I said, somewhat disturbed. "Just not all girls. Besides, she told me right up front to not expect anything, since she had a boyfriend in the Army."

"And you believed her?" said Helen "Maybe she was just playing hard to get."

"I don't play games," I said. "I tend to take everybody at face value. What they tell me, I believe."

"Well, you missed an opportunity," said Helen. "She wanted more, and really expected it from you. We talked about it all night. I think this was really her first date. The boyfriend is just a figment of her imagination."

"Not my problem," I said. "You are my best friend. Just don't ask me out on any more double dates."

None of these could be considered successful relationships, except Emma Lou.

All of these stories of me and other girls took place before I met Faye, except this one.

She was a good friend, pretty, and well-built, but seemed to have a permanent boyfriend—with whom she fought a lot. She and Joyce King did a tap dancing duet in most of our musicals. The boys in the shows couldn't keep their eyes off their skimpy costumes. Jewel was the art director for our school paper, and once when the Snoop column editor put in something about me having a crush on Jewel, which was not true, Jewel blew up. Didn't want her name in that column. I gently pointed out that the item was not about her, but about me, and I was the one to be offended. She cooled down, and apologized. We stayed friends, but no closer than that.

Apparently Jewel, and everybody else in school, learned of my rejection by Faye about the Press Banquet. One day she approached me, all friendly-like.

"Why don't you invite Joyce to the banquet," she said. "I think she would be pleased."

"Doesn't she have a boyfriend?" I asked.

"Yes, but he lives in Bristol, so she never gets to go to any school affairs."

I knew all Jewel wanted was to have her closest friend along for the affair, so what the heck, I asked Joyce and she agreed to go. It was a dull evening, since we were being polite to each other, but not nice.

CHAPTER FIVE, Emma Lou

But the only one of these relationships that showed promise was Emma Lou, and that died out too.

As I turned to sneak unobtrusively out of the schoolroom to avoid having to explain my presence, she turned her head towards me, straightened up, and asked, "Is there something I can do for you?"

Completely taken aback, I tried to worm my way out of an embarrassing situation by being funny. Awkward, but funny.

"Yes, you can go to a movie with me Saturday night," I cockily blurted out, knowing she would laugh at me and refuse, so that I could make my escape.

But she didn't!

Being on the staff of the high school newspaper, I had formed the habit of quite often spending my last study period of the day over in the pressroom, which was located in the basement of one of the two elementary school buildings. Then, sometimes I would go upstairs to one of the grade school rooms for a visit. Helen Mullins, one of the girls with whom I had attended school most of my life, often served as a substitute teacher when the first grade teacher was absent. There weren't enough qualified teachers to take up the slack, what with the war and all, so a high school student would be asked to fill in—if nothing else, just to baby sit the kids.

On this particular October day, after I had finished my projects in the pressroom, and, knowing that the first grade teacher was gone, I wandered up to her room, planning to talk to Helen. As I walked through the door, I saw immediately that the substitute teacher was not the one I expected to see. Bending over one of the students, with her back towards me, was a remarkably pretty girl with short dark hair. I recognized her as one who was a year behind me in school, but whom I had never met. She had the exceptionally fascinating name of Emma Lou.

"O. K.," she said, very nicely, in answer to my oh-so-stupid question, much to my surprise, consternation and pleasure.

"Aren't you interested in what is on?" I asked, still afraid that I hadn't heard right.

"No," she smiled. "Do you want me to meet you there?"

"No," I said, "I'll pick you up. I can drive my dad's car. Just tell me when."

"The Saturday afternoon matinee usually breaks at around six, doesn't it? Anytime before that would be O. K. Do you know where I live?"

"Yes. Why don't I come by at five, then we can stop in the drug store for something to eat or drink before the show?"

I went back down to the pressroom with mixed emotions. I had never really just come out and asked a girl for a date before. Oh, I went to school functions, sports events, and even to cast parties, after school plays and shows in which I had participated, with one girl or another—but this was a new experience for me.

When she came out of her house all prettied up in a nice skirt and sweater set, I was so delighted that I was momentarily apprehensive about telling her something I had planned to say. I had heard so many boys complain about girls wanting to do more than they could afford on dates, then being embarrassed by having to refuse. Although I had a good part time job, my resources for pleasurable spending were limited.

So, after telling her how nice she looked, and how

happy I was that she had agreed to go to the movie with me, I very carefully explained to her just how much money I had on me. It was more than enough for the drugstore refreshments before and after the show, plus the show admission itself—but it certainly wasn't going to buy any steak dinners. I had eaten at home, and presumed she had, too.

She surprised and pleased me by saying she really appreciated me telling her that, and then said, "All I really want is to go somewhere with you. I don't expect to be wined, dined and entertained."

I had planned to spend a little time with her in the drugstore, which had a soda fountain, where we could get all kinds of ice cream concoctions and soft drinks, plus some types of sandwiches. This was also where all the students hung out when they were downtown.

"You know, Emma Lou," I said, "I've never walked into that drugstore with a girl on an official date before. All the school people are really going to be shocked to see me coming in with one as pretty as you. Besides, I have not mentioned our date to anyone, have you?"

"No, just my family," she answered, sweetly, and then her mischievous nature showed itself. "This is a very popular movie, so there will be a big crowd in the drugstore when we get there. Let's go in acting like we have been secret sweethearts forever, and really shock them!"

So that's why we went hand-swinging through the door, laughing, talking—and watching all the heads jerk around and the whispering start. We found a vacant small two-person booth in back, where we wouldn't be crowded by anyone, and sat there for half an hour, holding hands, with eyes for each other only, then left to walk down to the theater, still holding hands. By now, of course, our talking and laughing was more about the reaction of the other students and parents, and even some of the teachers who had seen us.

After the show we went back to the drugstore, where several friends came over to talk to us, but we were still performing the same scenario, for the benefit of the friends. Except that by now I wasn't too interested in entertaining other people any more. It was getting to be for my pleasure, only. I didn't dare hope that Emma Lou felt the same way. On the way back to her home I found out.

Sliding over close to me in the car, she laid her head gently on my shoulder, and whispered, "I had fun tonight."

"Me too. I guess we put on quite a show."

"Even without that. That was fun, but I enjoyed us, too."

"I'm glad. Because that goes double for me."

"It's a little late," she said as we pulled up into the driveway of her folks' darkened house. "It looks like everyone's in bed. Maybe I'd better go on in."

I was a little disappointed that we were cutting a lovely evening short, but I complied with her wishes by opening the gate to their front yard and walking in with her. She reached for my hand just as we walked under a very large weeping willow.

"Uh, oh," I said, acting startled. "We're in trouble!"

"What's wrong?"

"This is a kissing tree," I explained, "and if a couple don't kiss when they are under it, it will fall on them!"

"Oh, my, we couldn't let that happen, now could we?" she said, turning towards me and sharing my embrace.

For the next few minutes we guaranteed that the old tree would never fall on us. We got way ahead of it, covering not only the present danger, but the past and future as well!

Over the next few months the other kids at school became accustomed to seeing us together, and pretty well ignored us. We shared no classes, so we could meet only before and after school, and at lunchtime. I had never been so happy in my life!

We never discussed anything serious, like even going steady, although I guess we could say we were. We just had a lot of fun, and some official dates. I thoroughly enjoyed the screwball things we did together, such as that day at the fairgrounds. As the school year was drawing to a close, and the weather became hot and humid, I found myself at some function there one afternoon, and she was there, too. Since her home wasn't too far away, I started walking there with her. Both of us were wet with perspiration, from our activities at the fairgrounds.

As we passed near one of the swimming holes nearby, she walked down to the riverbank and kicked off her sandals.

"Oh, no," I said.

"Oh, yes," she called back, as she jumped in, nice summer print dress and all!

So there was nothing for me to do but pull my shoes off, empty my pockets and follow her.

"Don't worry," she said, "our clothes will be dry by the time we get home!"

And she was right.

We had become so close that, like any other sixteen year old, I thought it would go on forever. But it didn't.

On the last weekend of school there occurred an annual event, the baccalaureate sermon for the graduating class, at one of the largest churches, and I was asked, or rather, told, to be an usher. Emma Lou was there, since her sister was graduating. She was always so very beautiful, even in a wet dress, but tonight, in a sheer white summer dress, showing off that dark brown hair, she was absolutely ravishing!

As I came by where she was sitting near the aisle, before the service started, she tugged at my sleeve.

"Will you take me home?" she asked, in her usual sweet way.

But did I detect an underlying negative note in her voice?

She hardly said anything at all, on the way home in the car. After we saw to it, for the thousandth time, that the kissing tree didn't fall on us, we stepped up on the porch.

"I won't see you any more," she said, almost matter-of-factly, as she looked away into the dark of the trees along the river.

"Why not?" I stammered, wondering what I had done wrong.

Here I had another whole year of high school, while she had two years. I had never given any thought at all to us not ever being us.

"My father has taken a job in a defense plant in Detroit," she said. "We are moving next week. He doesn't ever plan on coming back. He only waited this long so my sister could graduate."

"Then I'll come over and help you move. And we can certainly write to each other."

"No, I think we ought to say goodbye tonight. It's been great, being with you these last few months, but we both know that we are too young to get serious. I'll never forget you, but time and distance change people-and it will us, too."

I knew she was right.

There are many partings in everyone's life, but none are any harder than the first. As we said goodbye that night, between kisses, for the last time, I knew that she was leaving a hole in my heart that could never be filled, and I was not at all ashamed to have my tears intermingled with hers.

CHAPTER SIX, Grandma's Funeral

I had come home to my room from work at the factory in Dayton when my landlady called me to the phone. It was my sister.

"Grandma is dead," she said. "Can you come home? She had asked that her grandsons be pallbearers."

After getting the details of the funeral arrangements and schedules, I called the plant and headed for the bus station. There was good bus service all the way to Pennington. A bus from Dayton in the evening connected with one in Cincinnati, just fifty miles away, for Middlesboro, where a connecting bus for Pennington was available. So if you didn't mind spending the night on a bus, you could leave Dayton in the evening and arrive in Pennington early the next morning. This is what I proceeded to do.

The six hour bus ride across Kentucky gave me plenty of time to sleep, but I kept thinking that my grandma's death signified the end of an era. She had been born, she often told me, the year the Civil War ended—1865, I supposed. And she was the only grandparent I had ever known. my family, which was not noted for its closeness, still gathered wherever she was—and now, I thought, that would come to an end. There would be no central rallying figure, with her gone.

All of this left me with a feeling of sadness on the whole trip south—not just the loss of my grandma, but also the loss of the gathering of the clan. This meant that some of them would never see each other again. But even wakes can be full of surprises—and some of them happy surprises!

After arriving at my folks' place early in the morning, I cleaned up and headed for my uncle's house, where the wake, or "sitting up," was held. I liked this uncle and aunt—they were always pleasant to be around. And when you were at your lowest, my aunt could make you feel like a million dollars. Once, at age fifteen, when I was the least pleased with himself—pimples, size twelve shoes, broken front tooth and all—I showed up at her house in a new blue sport jacket and a burgundy tie.

"Boy, you sure are getting to be an old heartbreaker!" she told me.

I left her house on the hill that day without ever touching the ground! She was like that, a wise woman. And she was absolutely tireless and invaluable during times of stress and duress, like this wake. She spent all her time in the kitchen, making coffee, serving food, solving problems—no one knew when, if ever, she slept.

Sometime during the course of this evening, while reading, I dozed off on the couch. I didn't know how long I slept, but I was awakened by being hit in the face by a pillow. I opened my eyes to see standing before me, with an impish guilty grin on her face, the most beautiful girl I had ever seen. I threw the pillow back at her, she caught it and sat down beside me. It was Faye!

I hadn't seen her since high school—but I hadn't forgotten, anything—the form, the grace, the dark hair, and of course the eyes, the ever wondrous eyes!

She said she had been working in Tennessee, but was home now to stay. We fell to reminiscing about going to different schools, about her folks refusing permission for her to go to the press banquet with me. We laughed about the morning I delivered her graduation gift and caught her in her robe. Neither of us slept the rest of the night, and it passed so rapidly it seemed over almost instantly.

The next day was the day of the funeral, so we both had to go home and change clothes. We had to walk a mile down a dusty, dirty, slate-based road to the bus stop, but for me it was a country lane filled with clover, and lined with lilacs and roses. I floated down it about ten feet in the air. We agreed to meet back at my aunt's after the funeral that afternoon, since we couldn't be together at the service itself due to my duties as a pallbearer. I could feel her watching me all during the religious ceremony and the procession to the cemetery, and I couldn't wait to get back to the house to see her again.

As the day wore on, and family and friends were leaving, Faye had disappeared somewhere for a few minutes. I found myself alone out in the kitchen with my aunt.

Never looking up from the stove, she said, “Do you love that girl?”

Somehow the question did not even catch me by surprise.

“So much it hurts,” I said. “It’s really tearing me up inside.”

“Does she know it?” asked my aunt.

“Not unless she sees it in my eyes,” I answered.

“Then tell her.”

“I can’t.”

“Why not?”

“Because I’m not ready for anything like this, that’s why. Besides, I’m scared of how she might react.”

“Tell her and find out,” said my aunt. “I’ve been watching you both, and I know what I see.”

“O.K., suppose you are right,” I said. “What do I tell her? I love you, Faye, but that’s all I’ve got. This suit I’m wearing is the only one I own, and I just barely have a job. All I have is a head full of plans and a heart full of dreams.”

Then my dear aunt had said, “Tell her anyway. Girls have dreams, too, you know.”

But I didn’t, and I never did.

But I did promise to come back in two weeks, when I had to be in the area for my sister’s wedding, and I kept my promise—only to be sorry that I did.

CHAPTER SEVEN, Porch Visit

A bus trip, anywhere or anytime, is always a good time to dream. You are usually half asleep anyway, so your mind can relax and wander, rambling from one thought to another. And on the way back to Dayton, mine were all happy thoughts—thoughts of returning.

Did she really want me to? She said she did. Did I really want to? Did I tell my aunt the truth when I admitted my love for Faye? Or was I just caught up in the moment—a moment of death and sadness which I was trying to turn into one of life and happiness? Did I really believe that this girl could be a part of my life under any circumstances?

I had a long way to go in my dreams and plans, and I hadn't even thought about who, if anybody, might be sharing them with me. I felt that most of the girls I knew were already of marriageable age, and I wasn't, and none were interested in me anyway. And I sure was a long way from being ready, even if one was.

She had been so special at one time, and maybe the fascination had been brought back. Was it amplified in a time of peaceful death? But had it been turned into love, for either of us? I spent many hours during the next two weeks mulling over remembrances of each time they had been together. my heart jumped as each incident was recalled—school, basketball games, the drug store, the fair, the Baptist Church, the university—and that first time I had seen her sitting on her front porch banister in the moonlight, when I had innocently asked her brother who she was.

The disappointment later that year when her folks wouldn't let her go to the press banquet with me, which could have been the proudest moment of my life. Yet I understood. Faye and I had been only sixteen, and her parents were being protective. But now we were almost nineteen, and I had been around the world, while she had been a hundred miles from home working. We were quite grown up, and should be able to determine our own destiny.

I avoided new friends I had made in Dayton for the next two weeks, wanting to savor recent happenings to the utmost, while anticipating my return to even more happiness. I didn't even know what I was going to do. I just knew that I had said I would be back in two weeks and I meant to keep that promise.

I had always enjoyed porches—everyone I knew had one. My aunt's hung over the side of a hill—great view. My grandma's had faced the railroad "Y" across the creek, where, as a small boy, I used to watch the "Bristol" make its turn by pulling up along the hill, backing in behind St. Charles, then pulling forward to stop at the station. The porch at my own folks' place ran around two sides of the house, with two porch swings in place.

But my favorite porch was Faye's, and only because it held so many fond memories of me and her on it. Tonight was no exception. The moon, high above the mountains, was extremely beautiful—and so was she. The late evening, after we arrived back at her house, was so full of happy talk, laughter and enjoyment that I had no time to think of the future, or even where any of this might lead. I was just enjoying being alive and with her, and she seemed to be doing the same. We were not even sitting together or touching, yet I kept thinking what a wonderful, vivacious, interesting girl she still was.

At some point our visiting was disturbed by the front door opening and shedding some light from inside the house on the moonlit porch.

"Hi, Dad," she said.

I looked around to see her father standing there in just his pants, with the top of his underwear showing. When I started to greet her father, I was cut short.

"Get in the house, girl," ordered the man.

"Just a minute," she said.

"No, right now. And you, fellow, hit the road!"

As he re-entered the house, he hurled over his shoulder, "Don't be long. And you, young man, don't ever come back here again."

I leaned against the porch post, completely dumbfounded. Nothing like this had ever happened to me before. The parents of what few girls I knew seemed to like me better than their daughters did. I was scared to death, but couldn't figure out what I had done wrong.

I said, "I better go."

"Please don't," she said. "We can explain to him that we haven't done anything wrong."

"But for some reason he doesn't trust me. I don't have any choice."

I just didn't feel like trying to please both her and her family—especially since all of my thoughts regarding her were of the highest moral kind. I didn't think of her any other way, so it hurt to be distrusted. Here I was, a clean-cut young man, who did not smoke or drink, and had never been in jail. I did not understand her dad's attitude towards me at all.

"Then come back tomorrow," she said. "It will be alright then."

"I'm going back to Dayton tomorrow," I said, quietly.

"Please stay over another day," she pleaded. "Here you have a new blue suit and all!"

Even in the emotions of the moment I couldn't help but think of the incongruity of the remark. Just what did my new blue suit have to do with her father distrusting me? I realized she was grasping at straws.

"But Faye, I don't know how to handle this. I have to go away and figure it out."

"Oh, please don't go like this," she cried.

And the tears just poured from those heart wrenching blue eyes until I started to feel them rise in mine, too. Then it started to come up in my chest, a godawful throbbing pain that I knew would never stop until I died.

What was she trying to tell me? With my youth and naivete, I could only believe that she was embarrassed by her father's actions, and wanted to spare him. No way on god's green earth could it have been any feelings for me. Although in my wildest dreams I could never imagine her doing so, I knew underneath all this, in my heart, all she had to do was to utter three simple little words and she would alter the courses of their lives forever. But she didn't—and since the risk of further rejection was too strong, I didn't either.

I stepped over to her and held her close, all the while her tears were breaking my heart. I let her go and walked away towards the footbridge across the creek. In the middle of the bridge I turned around. She hadn't moved from the moonlit spot she was in, and I could almost see those wondrous blue eyes full of tears. And even though I had no idea what my next development might be, I knew those eyes would haunt me forever.

The temptation to race back to her, throw my arms around her, and tell her what my aunt had wanted me to was so great I had to bite my lip to hold back the tears.

But what if her tears were for her father, and not for me? No way could I stand that. I kept going.

CHAPTER EIGHT, Kingsport One

It was a warm September day when I flew into the Tri-cities Airport from Atlanta. Amidst the throes of creating another division of the company, and the accompanying increased travel involved. I had decided to take a couple of days and visit my mother in Kingsport on the way back to Chicago. When I realized that the Lee County Fair was scheduled for the following week, I decided to take an extra day and drive over from Kingsport. I hadn't been to that fair since the summer between my last two years of high school, when I had taken up tickets at the main gate. I convinced himself it was a good idea to take that kind of a break, since I was under more business pressure than I had ever had in my life.

I picked up my rental car at the airport, and spent the rest of the day with my mother. She told me that my cousin Howard and his wife had moved to Kingsport from Detroit, and bought a beauty shop—since they both had some training in the field of cosmetology. I couldn't imagine a big old boilermaker like Howard, a former professional baseball player, fixing women's hair—but then again, whatever trips your trigger.

The next day I left my motel early to drive out to Irwin, planning to have breakfast on the way. I had arranged a business meeting with an advertiser there, just so my side trip to that area would be legitimate. As I drove out through the south end of Kingsport, I had to go right past Howard's beauty shop—and there Howard was, going in the door. So I stopped. I hadn't seen

Howard since our grandmother died almost twenty years before, but my cousin hadn't changed much. It was Monday, so the business wasn't open, and since there was plenty of time, we did a lot of reminiscing.

In the course of discussing old friends who had moved away from Lee County, Howard said, "Did you know that Faye lives here now? Her brother and her folks moved here, and she and her daughter live with her folks."

I told Howard I had heard that she was widowed very early in her marriage, but that was all I knew. I had no idea why Howard had brought it up, and although my cousin and Faye's brother were the best of friends, I wondered how much, if anything, Howard knew about me and Faye.

"Yes," said Howard, "her husband remained in the Navy after the war, and I heard he died of a brain hemorrhage in an accident on his ship."

For the first time in almost twenty years an image was brought back—one that had been almost totally erased by other people and interests, just like the claustrophobia of the mountains had been erased by the wide open spaces where I had lived so long. An image that was at the same time both happy and sad. An image of a beautiful and vivacious, youthful and caring slip of a girl which suddenly changed to a memory of big beautiful blue eyes filled with tears, shining in the otherwise happy light of the full moon—and begging me not to go away.

As I went on and conducted my business in Irwin, I had difficulty concentrating on the tasks at hand, and by the time I got back to my motel, I had come to a joyful, yet, I knew, a dangerous conclusion. I had to see her again!

But what would I find? Like me, she would be only thirty-eight, but would she look old and care-worn? Would she be bitter because of what life had dealt her—soured on people, even old friends? No, I couldn't believe she would be anything except an older more mature extension of her old self. Perhaps still veiling her feelings, but I knew she would value old friendships. And that is why I wanted to see her—not to start anything, or to rekindle anything, real or imagined—but just to see for myself what she had become.

But how to do it? Just call her up? No, I didn't really want to meet her in a one-on-one situation. I would rather see her in a group. Not that I didn't trust himself—the stability of a way of life which I had spent twenty years developing for myself, and what was for me an excellent profession, certainly were strong competition for an ancient friendship in which I never knew how she really felt about me anyway.

Besides, hadn't I convinced himself twenty years before that I didn't love her? And that our whole relationship was out of balance? Her folks didn't like me, and she always gave me the impression that she was hoping that something better would come along. Right up until the night I said goodbye forever. But now, was forever to last only twenty years?

How could I see her again, and make sure we were not alone? Howard and Jean were out. I didn't know how much they knew, or suspected. And my mother was definitely out.

I kicked off my business suit after lunch and

sprawled on the motel bed to think about it. By the time I dozed off for a short afternoon nap I had it all figured out. Her folks! I would call her folks and invite them to have dinner with me, and if they accepted, I would casually suggest that they bring along their daughter and grand daughter. But I didn't think they would accept. Knowing the kind of people they were, I expected that they would invite me to their house instead, maybe even for dinner. Then I could see everybody again.

But what if they reacted negatively, refused my invitation and told him to get lost? Oh well, nothing ventured, nothing gained. I didn't think they would. They were older now, and they had always been hospitable people. After all, their dislike of me originally was only protectionism for their daughter. And I could understand that better now. A little while later, I woke up eager to make the call—but nothing ever goes the way you plan!

Just what had brought me to this point in my life, anyway? Why was I living a thousand miles from where I grew up? Why had I so little contact with old friends? Funny I should think of that at this time. I was never one to reminisce—much preferring the future to the past. Now here I was, twenty years later, in a motel room in Kingsport deliberately remembering the sequence of events and relationships that led me here.

Her mother's voice on the phone was nice and friendly, and, yes, she remembered me.

"We hardly ever eat out," she said. "Do you remember our daughter Faye? She's here. Why don't you talk to her?"

Do I remember her? She's all I've thought about all

day! That same sweet musical voice I used to worship was suddenly on the phone.

"Mom and Dad seldom go out to eat, but I would love to join you myself—anytime, anywhere!"

Just like that, right up front, she wanted to see me. No ifs, ands or buts. No stalling, no questions—just, "I would love to join you."

And I couldn't see anything wrong with that—two old friends visiting over dinner. No male-female relationship, just two old friends. And something told me she planned to keep it that way. I knew I did.

When she got out of her car I was standing in the entryway to the restaurant, and, even though it was almost twilight, I would have recognized her anywhere. The same graceful form in well fitting clothes, with every movement easy and comfortable—no nervousness, no hesitancy, self assurance at its best.

I met her about half way across the parking lot, and said, casually, "What would you do if I kissed you right here in front of all these people?"

"I'd kiss you right back," she said, smiling.

The kiss told me everything I needed to know. The feelings were still there!

"Hi," she said.

"Hi," I said. "That was a twenty year kiss."

Her laugh was as musical as I remembered it. It always sounded like the small rills trickling down the mountain sides near my boyhood home. And her eyes still had that blue—that deep blue that I used to fall in and swim around!

The dinner was uneventful, except for talk of what we had done for the past twenty years. She seemed really interested in my work, and indicated that she had no idea what had happened to me.

After I told her something of what an editor of an engineering magazine does, she said, "You seem to have gone so far, and I am still just little old Faye, here in the mountains."

"I could never think of you as just little old Faye!"

She then told me her folks were home and would like to meet me, so, leaving her car at the restaurant, we drove mine out to their house. Her mother and father were most pleasant hosts, and seemed glad to see me.

While being served chocolate cake and ice cream in the kitchen, ("We're informal people," she explained,) her father jokingly asked me if he had ever run me off from their house in St. Charles.

"Yes," I replied, "and it was the most traumatic experience of my life. I didn't understand the lack of trust, if that was what it was."

"You shouldn't have taken it personally," said her mother, laughing. "He ran everybody off at that time."

Faye just sat looking at her hands, her face a brilliant crimson. I could only guess at her thinking, now, as I had tried to twenty years ago.

This old boy might have changed two people's lives forever, I kept thinking, *and they're laughing about it.*

It was still a pleasant visit, and after awhile we returned to the restaurant to get her car. Her father voiced an opinion that he didn't understand why we left it there in the first place. Sitting in my car, alongside hers, in the parking lot, we continued our discussion, started on the way, of what had happened to whom—and the changes the years had brought in all our lives. Nothing personal, no discussion of us as us.

Then I said, "You know, Faye, in all the years we

knew each other, I never attempted to kiss you until today."

"And why was that?" she said. "Didn't you want to?"

"Yes, always, and I still do," I said. "I think I will now."

With that, I pulled her over to me in the car seat, and kissed her lovingly right on ther lips, and there was a full response. So I did it again. Soon we were like two teenagers in the car, hugging, kissing, smooching, continuously—but with no untoward advances from either of us.

Time passed so rapidly, as it usually does in like circumstances, that I was surprised when Faye suddenly said, "Oh my, it's midnight. I'd better get home."

Since there was no time for goodbyes, and I had discovered that her home was on the way to my motel, I suggested that I follow her and stop at her house for one last word. When she drove into the carport as I parked on the street, I didn't at first notice that the other car was missing. As I was walking up the driveway to where she waited, another car drove in.

"There's Dad," she said. "I wonder where he's been."

When her father got out of his car, she asked, almost casually, "Hi, where have you been?"

To which I replied, grumpily, "Looking for you. Get in the house."

"What?" she said, getting excited.

"Get in the house!" the man almost screamed at her. Then to her visitor, me, "You hit the road."

"Oh my god," she said. "I'll be in in a minute."

"A minute is all you've got," he said, and then to me, "I don't ever want to see you around here again!"

With that he went in the house.

"I'm a grown woman," she whispered, just loud enough to be heard. "But you'd think he didn't trust me."

"No, he trusts you. It's me he doesn't trust—and that still hurts just a little."

"Please don't leave like this," she begged, as I started for my car. "We can clear it up tomorrow."

I just stopped and looked at her.

"At least come back tomorrow," she said. "I don't want you leaving again feeling this way."

"I have no choice," I said, stepping close and putting my arms around her, "and neither do you."

And again I had this godawful pain in my chest, but this time I knew it was hurt for her, and what she must be going through, as again, I watched the tears well up in those soul-searing wonderful blue eyes in the light of the full moon. It all came back, as I backed away and left her standing on the step crying, as before, knowing I would never see her again.

The next morning, before I drove across the mountains to the fair at Pennington, I stopped at a florist in Kingsport and sent Faye a dozen red roses. The enclosed message read, "It's true. History sure as hell repeats itself!"

CHAPTER NINE, Goodbye for Now

After my tour of the fair and being surprised at how many people I knew, and knew me, I went back to Kingsport to visit my mother one last time before heading home. She informed me that Howard and Jean had been trying to reach me. It was late when I returned to my motel and called them.

"I'm glad you called," said Jean. "Faye has been trying all over to find you. She says she must speak to you before you leave town. You'd better call her."

"Not at this hour," I said. "It's too late."

"You'd better call her!"

The phone rang only once, and there was that voice again—but this time it was more serious than musical.

"I didn't want you to get away without apologizing for my father's actions, and to thank you for the roses."

"No thanks necessary, and no apology. He is still, in his own mind, protecting you, just as he did when you were eighteen."

"He is remorseful, telling me they should put him in an insane asylum. When are you leaving?"

"Early tomorrow. I have a flight to Louisville, then on to Chicago."

"I'll be there."

"Where?"

"At the airport, to see you off!"

As she drove up and parked, it occurred to me that I hadn't seen her in the daylight for over twenty years. She looked good—face beautiful, figure wonderful—as I should have expected—immaculately dressed, makeup perfect, every hair in place—and she was smiling. Again I assured her that no apology was necessary, and that none of this mattered to me—although I was still stinging underneath it all.

We stood in the early morning sunlight high up on the concrete walk overlooking the flight ramps—trying hard to avoid looking directly at each other. We made small talk about flying, the weather, the hills. Suddenly she was facing me.

"We can't go back twenty years, can we?" she said.

"No," I replied. "There have been too many changes, too many other people."

"What really went wrong with us?"

"I don't know," I lied, knowing full well that the main problem was weakness on the part of both of us—I was too weak to buck her folks, and she was too weak to tell me she really cared for me, if indeed she did.

I finally mustered up enough courage to look her right in the eyes. Oh god, those eyes—they soaked up my whole being, like a pair of beautiful blue sponges!

"Look, Faye," I said, "I love my way of life, immensely—there are other people in it. But at one time I thought I loved you, and I think you knew that. Maybe I still do. But this is an impossible situation."

"But you're not free. I wish you were, like I am!"

"Free?" I almost shouted. "Free? You have never been free! I am ensconsed in a situation which I alone created—people, a job, a part of the country in which I alone chose to live. And I was and still am free to direct my own life. But you don't know what freedom is. And you never will, until your folks are gone—and probably not even then!"

"Will I ever see you again?" she asked softly—her entire demeanor changing so that I immediately regretted my tirade.

"I don't know," I said, "Not in this world, maybe in the next, if there is one. But goodbye for now. They are boarding my flight."

As I chose my seat and relaxed on the plane, my brain started doing flip-flops among the events of the last few days, and the reminiscences of more than twenty years ago. Old habits never die, so I started mentally talking to myself.

"There could never be anything between us, then or now."

"I lied to my aunt twenty years ago. It was just the atmosphere of death that brought out that pseudo-love."

"Faye is a beautiful link to the past, but that is all."

Fifteen minutes later, as my plane made its takeoff roll, I could see her still standing on the walk—and I wondered again what was going through her head.

And that was the way I remembered her—whenever I thought of her at all.

CHAPTER TEN, Kingsport Again and Again

But a few months later, I found myself having to be in the Kingsport area again, so I brazenly called Faye and asked her to join me for dinner. She unhesitatingly said yes. Then I called Howard and Jean and invited them to join me, without telling them about Faye. After I picked the two of them up in my somewhat plush rental car, I simply announced that we had to go and pick up my "number one girl guide," who would join us for dinner, then I drove over to Faye's home. When I got out of the car and approached her front door, she came out, looking radiant as she always had.

"My folks aren't here," she said, almost casually. "They didn't want to see you again after our last meeting. They do not understand that we are doing nothing wrong—this is not a date. Just two old friends, almost forty, reminiscing. Their problem, not ours."

The evening was uneventful. Howard and Jean wanted to go to some dining area in Bristol that featured country ham, one of their favorites. Afterwards we went to their house for ice cream, then I drove Faye home—

nothing romantic about that, but I enjoyed being with her. It was somewhat sad for both of us, knowing we would never meet again. Slowly I wiped her out of my thoughts and memory. Was I ever really in love with her? I do not think so, but if I had wanted a girl from down home, it probably would have been her. But her family situation was impossible, yet maybe she would have left them if I had only encouraged her to. But I was not looking for any fights.

About a year later, my friend and business associate Jake and I had to be in Atlanta on business, so we stopped in Kingsport afterwards to play golf with Howard and Darrell. Besides, I wanted to show Jake where I came from. Since we were early for the golf game, I drove Jake in to the Sears store area where Faye worked in the office and introduce them. I don't know if he was impressed or not, but he seemed to agree that my life choices were the right ones.

CHAPTER ELEVEN, Final Analysis

When I was sixty-five, my mother's doctor called me to tell me she had been unconscious from a heart attack for some time, and wanted to know what to do. I told him I did not want him keeping her going with machines, if there was no hope. She lived a few days. I had gone to her home area of Kingsport a year before and pre-arranged everything with the funeral home, so there were no details to iron out. The wake was held one evening, and the funeral the next morning. As I was busy visiting with someone, some strikingly handsome woman came in and knelt by the casket—then turned and waved at me. I knew very few of my mother's friends, so I had no Idea who she was. Then when she approached me, I recognized her—Faye! Sixty-five, but still beautiful. She clasped my hand, and held on for several minutes. I politely visited with her and Darrell, who had accompanied her, and Howard, who had joined us. She did not come to the funeral the next day, and I finally realized that my connection with her, after some fifty years, was probably over.

Could we have ever been a couple? I do not think so, for many reasons. First, I never really knew how she felt about me. Perhaps she was looking for something better to come along. Second, her family's negative reaction to us being together. Was I not considered to be good enough for their little girl? Maybe no one was, but—at age twenty-three, pretty old for a girl's first marriage in that part of the world—she married a high school dropout, who had no job, so he joined the Navy. After he died in the Navy, she never remarried, probably because of the availability of a lifelong income from him. Third, and probably most important, I do not think she would have left her family and gone with me down that journey along the tough roads I had set out for myself. By the time she had gotten married, I had finished college on the G.I. Bill, had a good job as a manufacturing engineer, and had my first book published—a volume which brought me more income than her father made in his entire life!

But maybe I'm wrong. What if, when the first time her dad ran me off, I had asked her to return to Dayton with me, and she had gone? What if, during our closeness during my first visit back to Kingsport, when we were thirty-eight, I had decided to give up everything I had in order to make her mine, and asked her to be mine at that time? I’ll never know—because I was just not ready for anything like that at any of those times. My feelings for her were never that strong.

THE END

www.ingramcontent.com/pod-product-compliance
Ingram Content Group UK Ltd.
Pitfield, Milton Keynes, MK11 3LW, UK
UKHW041905190726
13854UKWH00003B/1096

9 781365 141195